FACET BOOKS

HISTORICAL SERIES

FACET fb BOOKS

HISTORICAL SERIES—22
(Reformation)

Charles S. Anderson, Editor

Luther and the Peasants' War

by HUBERT KIRCHNER

translated by Darrell Jodock

FORTRESS PRESS   PHILADELPHIA

This study was first published in Heinrich Foerster, ed., *Reformation Heute* (Berlin and Hamburg: Lutherisches Verlagshaus, 1967), pp. 218–47, and is republished by arrangement with the author and the publisher.

Published by Fortress Press, 1972

Library of Congress Catalog Card Number 73–171507

ISBN 0–8006–3068–8

Introduction

EVEN in the tumultuous sixteenth century the Peasants' War of 1524–25 was of major importance. While it did not directly involve the great powers, such as Charles V, Francis I, and Suleiman, and was only of short duration, it did affect in a significant way the course of German history generally and the Reformation specifically.

The rebellion of 1524–25 was only one in a long series of protests. Contributing factors were concrete grievances like economic and political repression, but also less tangible elements: the new self-image of the peasant and the winds of religious reform. The protest originated in South Germany in 1524, spread quickly to other parts of the country, and then was put down just as quickly when the farmers and tradesmen found themselves no match for the professional soldiers of the rulers. Only two years earlier the rebellious knights had been crushed; now the peasants suffered the same fate.

Although the literature on the subject of the Peasants' War is voluminous, there is no agreement on how the uprising is to be interpreted. For example, the Weinsberg Massacre conjures up images of the radical bloodthirsty nature of the peasants; on the other side, the Battle of Frankenhausen illustrates the harshness of the princes. Most casual discussions of the war center on the excesses of one side or another, documented by the events of Weinsberg or Frankenhausen. To some, the only point of significance has to do with Luther's passionate denunciation of the revolt. Here, at last, they feel they see the Saxon in his true colors. For others, the whole event is seen as an early rising of the proletariat, led by heroes of early communism.[1]

However we interpret the uprising, it is clear that it had serious consequences for the Reformation movement. Conservative theological and political polemicists insisted that the rebellion was a necessary result of the Reformation. This criticism confirmed some of the upper classes in their opposition to the Reformation. On the other hand, large numbers of the lower classes, angered by that part of Luther's response which urged the rulers to repressive action, turned away from the Saxon, either to return to the Roman Catholic fold or to become a fertile seedbed for the Anabaptists. Lutheranism became a middle and upper-class movement.

The author of the essay before us begins by analyzing briefly the background, the causes, and the sequence of events in the rebellion. He then turns to sources which Luther used in arriving at his position regarding the tumult. The major portion of the article follows and deals with the stance Luther adopted, seen in its historical and theological context.

The article is particularly helpful in its emphasis on the *Admonition to Peace*, which represents Luther's considered opinion, rather than stressing the more frequently quoted *Against the Robbing and Murdering Hordes of Peasants*. The central issue for Luther was theological, not political, and it was related to exegesis of certain parts of Scripture rather than to a careful analysis of contemporary events. His basic attitude

1. Cf. M. M. Smirin, *Die Volksreformation des Thomas Müntzer und der Grosse Bauernkrieg* (Berlin, 1956) for a review of various Communist treatments. See also Karl Kautsky, *Communism in Central Europe in the Time of the Reformation* (London, 1897), Manfred Bensing, *Thomas Müntzer und der Thüringer Aufstand 1525* (Berlin, 1966), and Josef Macek, "Zu den Anfängen des Tiroler Bauernkrieges," *Historica*, I (Prague, 1959), pp. 135–95; "Das Revolutionsprogram des deutschen Bauernkrieg vom Jahre 1526," *Historica*, II (1960), pp. 111–44; and *Der Tiroler Bauernkrieg und Michael Gaismair* (Berlin, 1965).

was one of sympathy for the peasants; and yet, as the author shows clearly, the Reformer moved gradually to the point where he viewed the rebellion as a demonic manifestation, a part of the last times.

The final section critically examines Luther's position. The author discusses Luther's failure to instruct the princes on their Christian duty as he had the peasants, his generalization—on the basis of limited data—about the place of "enthusiasm" in the movement, and his adoption of a theological stance which was based on a lack of clarity regarding the actual situation. By contrast, some of the other reformers, e.g., Urbanus Rhegius and John Brenz, acted more constructively. In summary, the author argues that Luther missed the opportunity to be the mediator and expert which both sides needed.

The essay was delivered at a theological conference sponsored by the Lutheran World Federation in East Berlin from May 29 to June 2, 1967. Hubert Kirchner is a young theologian from the German Democratic Republic (D.D.R.). His lecture has been published in *Reformation Heute: Bibelarbeit und Referate auf der internationalen Theologentagung des Lutherischen Weltbundes vom 29.5 bis 2.6 1967 in Berlin*, edited by Heinrich Foerster. It was published in 1967 by the Lutherisches Verlagshaus, Berlin and Hamburg.

CHARLES S. ANDERSON

Luther Theological Seminary
St. Paul, Minnesota
Fall, 1971

LUTHER AND THE
PEASANTS' WAR

It is quite obvious that the topic "Luther and the Peasants' War" is of key importance within the structure of the general theme of this conference. There is no need to justify its inclusion. Not only does the Peasants' War of 1525 form a particularly salient point in sixteenth-century German history, it also constitutes an important break in the history of the German Reformation. Not many other events in this period that were as secular as the Peasants' War affected the theological development as strongly as it did. On the other hand, it is widely regarded as an indisputable fact that the judgment of theologians has seldom influenced the outcome of a historical movement to the degree that it did in the Peasants' War. Various disciplines, consequently, have always been concerned with the relationship between the Reformation and the Peasants' War. Historians and theologians alike have devoted themselves to this problem with an intensity that is reserved for only a few special questions; yet it is still not possible to claim that an adequate conclusion has been reached. In the writing of secular history especially, the new assessment of sociological and social questions in our day has meant that increased attention is being given to the social movements in history. This reassessment has affected church history as well. If church history, as a theological discipline, is unable to shut its eyes to questions of general interest, how much less can it avoid dealing with those questions which are burning in the realm of theology itself. Thus the topic of the "Peasants' War" and the particular theme of "The Reformation and the Peasants' War" has become a burning issue again and cannot be dismissed by reference to the abundance of pertinent publications already available. The topic has not been disposed of, and it will not be settled so quickly.

The only question is whether it can still be given its traditional formulation. To ask about *Luther's* relation to the Peasants' War, is to draw limits and abandon terminologically the overarching theme of this whole session: *"Reformation* and Society." In this distinction—the question about the Reformation over against the question about Luther—a factual judgment is already strongly implied, namely, that when one has described Luther's relation to the Peasants' War the attitude of the Reformation as a whole has been described as well. A closer look at the matter, however, shows that this cannot be. If we wanted to speak more precisely about this, we would have to make use of the intensive historical investigation of Luther and his co-workers which has been undertaken recently.

All the same, I do not on my own want to broaden the subject given me. The question of Luther's relation to the Peasants' War is still important. Even if Luther's attitude was neither the only one nor the most detailed, it was still the one most effective in its time. Therefore, limiting the topic to him is amply justified. I hope you will permit me to hint, at least, at the larger context in a short concluding glance at the opinions of the Peasants' War held by other reformers. That larger context could not be encompassed within the scope of an essay like this one anyway.

In a first section, Part I, I want to consider briefly the background, the causes, and the historical sequence of events. I think that I can make it short. The general outline will be familiar to you. It is necessary only to recall it once again. A second section, Part II, will be devoted to the sources, both those which Luther used in judging the situation and those others we use in judging Luther's position. The sections which follow are the most important, however: Parts III and IV. Part III will contain the main body of the exposition. There I will deal first with the question of why and under what circumstances Luther took the position he did in respect to the Peasants' War, and second with the point of view he expressed in this context. Here too I will have to be extremely selective of course, especially in regard to the quotations. I cannot report on the contents here but must trust that the main outlines of Luther's writings about the Peasants' War are familiar to you. In Part IV, finally, I will attempt to examine somewhat critically Luther's attitude as a whole. This is also a point that distinguishes us, in part, from our ancestors and to that degree entitles us to consider this topic anew. We believe that it is no longer necessary to agree with Luther in every instance. In the context of Part IV we will also find an opportunity to take the already mentioned sidelong glance at the attitudes of the other reformers. Perhaps this too will provide us with criteria for judging the opinions of Luther.

I

A. Early in the summer of 1524 the Stühlingen peasants revolted against their lords when the countess, in the middle of harvest, required them to gather snails' shells on which she wanted to wind yarn. This revolt, as it were, gave the signal for a general insurrection, yet the revolt did not come out of the clear blue sky. The peasants who revolted only threw the torch into kindling wood which had been prepared a long time beforehand. Decades had labored to accumulate this kindling and had tested its combustibility from time to time. In Switzerland, in Alsace, in Southwest Germany, in Central Austria there had been more than one riot not only of the peasants but of all the lower classes. Several factors combined to make this entire region particularly susceptible to social upheaval.

history of previous revolts

3

So, to mention only the most important centers of upheaval before the general insurrection, there had been the Swiss peasants' war in 1513–15; it was fought under the symbol of the *Bundschuh* and was one of the last crescendos in the struggle over the old law. The peasants, who had come together from various regions, demanded that all "new regulations (*Aufsätze*)" be abolished and that the country "stay with its old custom and justice."[1] At the same time as the Swiss uprising and not unrelated to it, the "Poor Conrad" movement arose in Württemberg in 1514. Somewhat later, in 1517, there arose the *Bundschuh* movement in the Upper Rhine under Joss Fritz. Twice before—in 1502 in the bishopric of Speyer and in 1513 in a fief in Breisgau—he had sought in vain to change social conditions radically under the sign of the *Bundschuh* and with the slogan "Nothing but the righteousness of God," which was emblazoned on the conspirators' flag above the crucifix. In the past treason had always destroyed Fritz's plans and preparations, and this time, too, the lords were informed before the storm could break loose.

The points at issue in these uprisings were mainly questions of law—the restoration of the original laws or the production of new, loftier legal norms. Overt material and economic questions likewise played a role, but not the decisive one. In the cities, for example, political opposition to the oligarchic administration was also a factor. None of these elements may be separated from the others. Somehow they all converged, although the mixture was different in each particular locality.

In 1524–25, the general social situation was not such that bitter necessity caused the peasants to take up arms. Certainly there were regional differences. Serfdom with its wide-reaching personal restraints and multifarious shameful results still existed in large sections of Germany. The division of property [through inheritance], again especially in Southwestern Germany, had led to the formation of households so small as to be hardly

1. According to G. Franz, *Der deutsche Bauernkrieg* (Darmstadt, 1956), p. 9.

capable of sustaining themselves; and an accelerating monetary depreciation, combined with a mounting debt on the farms, also made material cares more threatening. In addition there was the especially annoying economic practice of the monasteries who, like the church in general as the largest landholder, used both force and excommunication to advance their vested interests. The situation was entirely confused because of territorial fragmentation. This fragmentation not infrequently resulted in great local uncertainty for the subjects, because several lords would press their claims at the same time. Yet all of this was still not the finally decisive factor in 1525.

Quite often it was the well-to-do peasants who led the insurgents. They were joined by craftsmen and a not inconsiderable portion of the citizens from the cities, some of whom followed the movement very willingly. Even representatives of the lower nobility, who could be encountered among the peasants, had not all simply bowed to external pressure. Something greater and loftier was at stake than mere daily bread. It was more a matter—expressed or unexpressed, known or unknown —of the social recognition of the fourth estate, of the peasantry in general.

The peasant was beginning to recognize himself. The self-designation, "Poor Conrad," already shows this. Here those who were originally intended to be insulted by the designation consciously picked it up and elevated it to a name of honor. In much the same way the clumsy footwear of the peasant, the *Bundschuh,* was made their insignia. The peasant was no longer the one to be despised by all.

The popular writer Eberlin von Günzburg, later also a preacher in the front lines of the Reformation, closed the sixth of his fifteen *Bundesgenossen,* years before the general insurrection occurred, with the designation: "The peasant is becoming sly."[2] This sentence could almost be designated as the motto of the entire Peasants' War. Although Luther may have

2. J. E. von Günzburg, *Ausgewählte Schriften,* Flugschriften aus der Reformationszeit, vol. 11 (Halle, 1896), p. 65.

been right when he protested that it was slander to make him the father of the Peasants' War, as Roman Catholic polemic liked so very much to do even long after the suppression of the riots, we cannot overlook the fact that his proclamation of the freedom of the Christian man, his criticism of the church, and the social and national notes of his great Reformation writings all fell as fertile seeds into well-prepared ground. These seeds, however, did not all produce the fruits which their sower had intended.

B. With regard to the external course of events, I will content myself essentially with a few figures. Early in the summer of 1524 the peasants of the territory of Stühlingen rioted for the reasons already mentioned. The occasion was trivial enough, but it released a long accumulated fury towards a heavily indebted government which believed it could demand anything from its subjects. Despite the preparations made by both sides, no actual battles occurred. The peasants received the assurance of a free court of arbitration for their grievances and a legal basis for their existence. In principle, that could have settled everything. But the example was instructive. What had been guaranteed to one could only appear as reasonable for others. And thus by the beginning of the new year things began to happen in a hurry. Already during Christmas of 1524 the Baltingers in Upper Swabia revolted, in January it was the subjects of the chapter house at Kempten, in February a band of peasants was formed at Lake Constance.

All three bands operated in close contact with one another and entered into negotiations with the Swabian League, the military arm of the governments in the region. At the beginning of March, the soon to be famous "Twelve Articles" were formulated. By the middle of March they appeared in print and were circulated very widely. At the same time the Memmingen Articles were drafted and made the basis for negotiations with the city council, negotiations which did in fact have positive results. In April one region after the other joined in. The stage of purely regional negotiations with the lords was long since past. Soon weapons spoke the last word. In part the lords had been clever enough to delay the proceedings until their preparations were at a point where they would be able to begin the battle with a prospect of success and would no longer be dependent upon scandalous negotiations with their own subjects. As a result of their own negligence, the element of surprise and the numerical superiority of the peasants, the lords had lost several encounters in the first assault. Time, however, was working against the peasants.

By April all of South Germany was astir. The outermost limits of the movement lay approximately at the western boundary of Alsace on the west, at the Köln–Magdeburg line on the north, the Leipzig–Zwickau line on the east, and on the south the boundary was formed approximately by Lake Constance and the River Lech up to the Danube. It can therefore be said that about one-third of the area then dominated by German culture had been gripped by the insurrections. The main center evidently lay in the Upper German region. Here is where the decisive documents such as the Twelve Articles were formulated; here also is where there emerged the most comprehensive conceptions of a desired new social order.

In addition the following particulars should still be mentioned: On April 16 there occurred the so-called Weinsberg Affair, in which a number of lords with their servants, who had not been killed in the struggle for the city, were hunted down; one day later, on April 17, at another place the treaty at Weingarten was made between the Swabian League and the Lake Constance Association (*Seehaufen*). During the first week of May, Müntzer with his men moved through Eichsfeld. On May 4–5 there ensued the Amorbach Explanation by the Neckartal band and the summoning of the "Peasants' Parliament" at Heilbronn. In the middle of the month this parliament met to consider among other things, Friedrich Weigand's plans for imperial reform. However, real consultations were no longer achieved.

May 15 witnessed both the battle at Frankenhausen and

Müntzer's arrest; on May 27 he was executed. The battle at Zabern on May 17 meant the end of the Peasants' War in Lothringia. On May 25 Mühlhausen was taken. The story was the same at one place after another. Almost every encounter now ended with a defeat for the peasants. The series of dates could be extended beyond May, but by May the outcome of events was no longer in doubt. Despite new attempts at insurrection in various localities, the peasants' defeat had been sealed. In any case the attitudes of the Reformers were shaped in these early months, so the further outward developments no longer play a role in their assessment.

II

A. What did Luther know of all this? By reading his writings and especially his sermons it can in general be established over and over again that he was informed amazingly well and quickly. In exceptional cases the sources for his information are even specifically mentioned: letters, writings by others which he received, or also visits which are known to have taken place. A great deal must have traveled from mouth to mouth as well as via couriers who were really traveling for other purposes.

Thus also in the case of the Peasants' War we must reckon with better information than can be reliably documented. Luther was, of course, acquainted with the Twelve Articles of the Upper German peasants, to which he responded with the *Admonition to Peace*.[3] He was also familiar with the Weingarten treaty made between the Swabian League and the Lake Constance Association (*Seehaufen*) on April 17. He regarded it as so important, as such a positive model of the desired peaceful settlement of the conflict, that he had it reprinted once more,

---

3. For the Twelve Articles, see A. Götze and L. E. Schmitt, *Aus dem sozialen und politischen Kampf,* Flugschriften aus der Reformationszeit, vol. 20 (Halle, 1953); English translation in *Luther's Works,* American Edition, Philadelphia and St. Louis (hereafter referred to as *LW*), vol. 46, pp. 8–16. See also Luther's "Ermahnung zum Frieden," *Luthers Werke,* Weimarer Ausgabe (hereafter referred to as *WA*), vol. 18, pp. (279) 291–334; *LW* 46, 17–43.

in the beginning of May, supplied with a preface and an epilogue.[4] And it must be assumed, thirdly, that he was acquainted with the so-called Memmingen Agreement of March, 1525.[5] This document closed with a list of experts in the divine law to which the peasants were appealing. This list is illuminating enough. It consists exclusively of the names of theologians from both great camps of the Reformation; at the top stand the names Luther and Melanchthon. At the beginning of his *Admonition to Peace,* Luther alludes to this document and the inclusion of his name.[6] Moreover, Luther was acquainted, of course, with Thomas Müntzer's writings. He also knew generally about the events in Mühlhausen and Thuringia. This knowledge came in part from his own highly discouraging experience, for Luther himself was in Thuringia from April 16 to May 6, and by means of his personal intervention in various localities, he attempted to salvage whatever there was to salvage. The purpose of his trip was really to establish a new Latin school in Eisleben, the direction of which was to be in the hands of Johann Agricola. Luther, however, ventured out from Eisleben on various excursions into the riot-torn areas. He was certainly in Stolberg, later in Wallhausen, Nordhausen, Weimar, and Seeburg. He preached on several occasions, but he was unable to accomplish anything and finally had to be content with escaping uninjured. The angry crowd hissed him. It goes without saying that these bitter experiences were reflected in his written judgments.[7]

What additional sources of information Luther may have had access to remains uncertain. We can hardly assume that still more written documents, peasants' articles or the like, came into his hands. In that case we would expect some kind of reference

4. *WA* 18, (335) 336–43.

5. H. Boehmer, ed., *Urkunden zur Geschichte des Bauernkrieges und der Wiedertäufer,* Kleine Texte für theologische und philologische Vorlesungen und Übungen, vol. 50–51 (Bonn, 1910; Berlin, 1933), pp. 22–24.

6. *WA* 18, 292, *ll.* 1–3/20 f.; *LW* 46, 17.

7. Concerning the course of the journey and the particular stops along the way, cf. *WA* 17$^\mathrm{I}$, xxxi f.

to them beyond the one general hint which perhaps could be mentioned in passing.[8] None of these possibilities can be excluded. Nevertheless in our assessment of the situation we cannot—and this alone is what matters—proceed beyond what can be said with certainty.

B. For an assessment of Luther's position in and towards the Peasants' War, six specific publications from his own pen are available as sources. (1) In the first place there is the treatise which we have mentioned several times already, his *Admonition to Peace*,[9] written at the end of April during his trip to Thuringia. It certainly was begun in Eisleben and quite probably was written down all at once, for there is still no reflection of his bad experiences there. The *Admonition* is marked by its relatively factual tone and the pains taken to approximate justice in its treatment of both sides. (2) During this journey, Luther must also have written the prologue and epilogue to the Treaty of Weingarten, which had first appeared in print on April 22. An exact date, however, cannot be established.[10] (3) Immediately after his return on May 6, Luther must have begun composing the manifesto *Against the Robbing and Murdering Hordes of Peasants*.[11] This treatise is completely under the spell of his experiences on that journey and actually has those experiences alone in view, although of course it is dependent on general theological principles. In view of that fact alone it is regrettable that this manifesto has been regarded as the representative judgment by Luther on the Peasants' War. It is by no means typical. However, Luther himself sowed the seeds of this misunderstanding. The first edition, to which only more recent investigations have called attention,[12] was published together with a new edition of the *Admonition to Peace* and was

8. *WA* 18, 299, *ll.* 13/31; *LW* 46, 23.

9. See above, note 3.

10. See above, note 4.

11. *WA* 18, (344) 357–61; *LW* 46, 49–55.

12. K. Aland, " 'Auch wider die reuberischen und mörderischen rotten der anderen bawren,' Eine Anmerkung zu Luthers Haltung im Bauernkrieg," in *Theologische Literaturzeitung* 74 (1949) : 299–303.

set apart from it only by means of a new title. That new title was supposed to distinguish between peasants and peasants with the distinctive wording: . . . Also *Against the Robbing and Murdering Hordes of the* Other *Peasants*. But the formulation of the title alone proved to be too weak for that purpose. Printing the two treatises together could also indicate very easily that both were addressing identical groups. This danger was evident as soon as the first reprints appeared. None followed the pattern of the first edition. All of them separated the two treatises. At the same time all omitted from the title of the second treatise the two words which indicated its relationship to the first treatise. The two words now had become meaningless, although the differentiation depended on them alone. In this way the special thrust of the appeal was lost and it was given a general validity like that of the *Admonition to Peace*. Such general validity had not been intended at all. (4) On the imprisoned Müntzer a satchel with letters had been found. Luther learned about them from his Mansfeld friends. In order to support his own assessment of Müntzer's spirit and intention, Luther published during the second half of May a selection of these letters together with his commentary. It was entitled *A Dreadful Story and a Judgment of God Concerning Thomas Müntzer*.[13] (5) and (6) The dismay over the appeal *Against the Robbing and Murdering Hordes of Peasants* was universally great. Even Luther's friends asked him to add a commentary. Some even demanded that he apologize formally for having here greatly exceeded the bounds of what was commanded and permitted. For a long time Luther resisted this pressure. In a Pentecost sermon on June 4, which has been handed down primarily in a transcription by Stephan Roth,[14] he reacted explicitly and harshly against his critics. He must nonetheless have eventually been convinced that there was still a final, genuinely public word to be spoken. Therefore in the middle of July he wrote *An Open Letter on*

13. *WA* 18, (362) 367–74.
14. *WA* 17^I, (xl f.) 265–67.

the Harsh Book Against the Peasants.[15] It was a detailed encounter with the arguments of his opponents from the most diverse camps. This was really his last public statement. To be sure, Luther later still made statements from time to time about the events of 1525. The words and deeds of Thomas Müntzer were often cited as a paradigm. Even with increasing historical distance, however, nothing changed in his judgment of the peasant insurrections. Even in Luther's later years, he did not retreat from his former position.

III

A. The immediate occasion for Luther's public statements during the Peasants' War was the appeal specifically addressed to him by the peasants. The above mentioned list of the solicited experts on the divine law contains fourteen names. Of these men Luther was the only one who felt the appeal strongly enough to react with an opinion concerning the Twelve Articles. To be sure there were still others from the list who issued an expert opinion concerning the course of events and the submitted Articles in particular. For example, Melanchthon and Brenz, Zell from Strassburg, and the two other preachers from that city, Capito and Bucer—to name just a few—all wrote on this subject. But all of them had different reasons for writing; Melanchthon and Brenz, for example, wrote at the request not of the peasants but of their prince, Ludwig of the Palatinate.

Luther explained why he wrote his *Admonition to Peace*: "Since I have a reputation for being one of those who deal with the Holy Scriptures here on earth, and especially as one whom they mention and call upon by name in the second document, I have all the more courage and confidence in openly publishing my instruction. I do this in a friendly and Christian spirit, as a duty of brotherly love."[16] The topic was set, since the peasants had published their Articles with scriptural passages in the

15. *WA* 18, (375) 384–401; *LW* 46, 63–85.
16. *WA* 18, 291, *ll.* 14/27–292, *ll.* 5/22; *LW* 46, 17.

margins as proofs. At the same time, however, they had also asked to be instructed further from Scripture. This pleased Luther the most. For then there was still hope that the whole affair would turn out well. In any case he did not want to remain silent and by means of this silence perhaps promote something from which immeasurable harm might emerge.

Luther did not thereby directly specify what was the central problem in the relationship of the riots and their documents to the Reformation. This is only suggested. In the course of Luther's explanations it became completely clear, however: the peasants are appealing to the gospel. In the margin of the printed Twelve Articles there stand an abundance of Bible passages, which are to prove that their demands are rooted in divine law. The Memmingen articles of union (*Bundesordnung*) begin with the words: "The Christian association and union was begun in order to praise and honor the almighty, eternal God, to exalt the holy gospel and the divine word, as well as to support justice and the divine law; it was not begun in order to defy or handicap anyone, clergy or layman, who supports and accepts the gospel, but is especially for increasing brotherly love."[17] And the list at the end, which enumerates those experts who should be appealed to concerning the divine law, proves clearly what was meant here by divine law: the gospel of the youthful reformation movement. Here the attempt is being made to tie the concerns of the peasants to those of Luther. The question now is: Is this legitimate or not? And further: What is the response from the Reformation which has been appealed to in that way? It is Luther's incontestable merit that he recognized the fundamental significance of this problem and that he was the only one who tackled the issue on that fundamental level without having been commissioned to do so by a third party or for any limited purpose. Everyone, of course, recognized the issue. But no one began to elaborate it beyond the limits of his own responsibility. Luther was the only one who clearly rec-

17. W. Zöllner, ed., *Zur Geschichte des grossen deutschen Bauernkrieges. Dokumente und Materialien* (Berlin, 1961), p. 60.

ognized that the situation itself already demanded an answer from the Reformation party which had been appealed to in that way. This answer he gave with his *Admonition to Peace*. It is not certain whether Luther knew that the most important document of the insurrection was the Twelve Articles he held in his hands and that they alone were worth answering, because we do not know whether he was acquainted with additional petitions of grievances. In any case, however, the most general and therefore also the most important document did in fact lie before him, and to that degree his answer could also claim for itself a general validity.

On the basis of these considerations and the opinion already mentioned (i.e., that the appeal *Against the Robbing and Murdering Hordes of Peasants* bears the stamp of exceptionally negative experiences and does not accurately reflect Luther's attitude), I want to refer principally in the following analysis to the *Admonition to Peace*. It also was not written *sine ira et studio* ["without wrath and zeal"] but is nonetheless not overly harsh. To this degree, it is best suited to clarify the foundations of Luther's intention and his judgments.

B. (1) If we do not want from the very beginning to block our every access to understanding Luther's attitude, the first thing we must keep in mind is the fact that Luther wrote as a theologian, even in the writings aimed at the peasants' uprisings. And he wanted his judgments to be correspondingly theological. That has often been denied Luther; it was denied already in his own time, and the voices have not grown silent even in our own day. But treating him seriously as a theologian, as a doctor of the Holy Scriptures, really has nothing to do with "idealistic, metaphysical blinders," nor does it mean "raising dust clouds of religious mysticism," as has been asserted again recently;[18] it simply means taking Luther seriously at the one place where he wanted to stand. Everyone is, of course, a child of his age. Everyone lives in the surroundings peculiar to him,

18. G. Fabiunke, *Luther als Nationalökonom* (Berlin, 1963), pp. 9 f.

whose forming influence he cannot avoid. Each person's thinking, willing, and acting, at least in their fundamentals, are imprisoned in the intellectual and material situation of his time.
This is true of Luther as well. But it is a truism, and there is in
reality no real antithesis. To understand and evaluate Luther
and his work theologically does not mean tearing him from his
root-soil, but it does mean understanding him at that place
where alone he can be understood, if he is to be understood at
all. Luther was no politician. He never was one, not even when
he took a position on a political question, and consequently also
not in the Peasants' War. In his Table Talk he once emphasized: *"Christus non curat politiam aut oeconomiam."*[19] That
was no christological assertion, but rather a confession also
valid for Luther himself. In short, at stake here is also a question concerning the implementation of his doctrine of the two
kingdoms. Luther understood that he had been asked as a
theologian, as "one of those who deal with the Holy Scriptures
here on earth,"[20] as he stated at the beginning of his *Admonition to Peace.* As such a man he answered. And when he saw
himself confronted by such a broad front of rejection, he did
not hesitate to emphasize once again in his *Open Letter*: "I . . .
want . . . to be concerned only about what God's word requires.
On this basis, my little book was and remains right, even
though the whole world take offense at it."[21]

The reproach that Luther in the Peasants' War showed himself to be the great servant of the princes runs along the same
lines. This formulation also is of recent vintage, but it has its
earlier prototypes. Already in his anti-Lutheran *Highly Necessary Defense and Answer Against the Spiritless, Soft-Living
Flesh in Wittenberg* (1524), Müntzer for example called
Luther a "flattering scoundrel," who "plays up to the godless

19. *WA* Tischreden 1, 470, no. 932.
20. *WA* 18, 291, *ll.* 14 f./27 f.; *LW* 46, 17.
21. *WA* 18, 386, *ll.* 17–19; *LW* 46, 66. Cf. also Luther's sermon from
May 12, 1525: "Christianus praedicator non curat, quod sibi adhaerentur,
sed quia verbum dei praedicat," *WA* 17^I, 237, *ll.* 5 f.

scoundrels (i.e., the princes)."[22] Several years later Luther himself said that the "papists" had reproached him in the same way even earlier, because he was always dealing with spiritual subjects only and not with temporal ones as well.[23] No witnesses can be found to substantiate this, however. But after the Peasants' War such terms became rather common. It was reported from Leipzig that people there were saying Luther feared for his life, because Elector Frederick the Wise had died and, therefore, was playing up to (i.e., flattering) Duke George in part to assure himself of a new temporal protection.[24] And Cochlaeus, Luther's most bitter Roman Catholic opponent, did not miss this opportunity for polemics; he called Luther simply a "flatterer of princes" [*principum fautor*].[25]

This reproach refers to Luther's continuing acceptance of the existing governmental system despite all criticism; it refers to his acknowledgment of the authority of the princes as well as his striving to maintain them as given by God and to strengthen them with the admonition: Whoever refuses obedience to the princes, refuses it to God, even when the authorities are guilty of illegal encroachments on their subjects. Even then it is better to suffer for the sake of order, as suffering befits a Christian, than it is to defend oneself. Therefore every riot is to be understood a priori and on principle as directed finally against God and is to be judged in the same way, no matter how many arguments for an objective vindication may be introduced.

Neither cheap opportunism nor a desired (*dezidiert*) political program, however, drove Luther to this point of view. The driving force was nothing else than the Holy Scriptures, more specifically the text in Romans 13, 1 Peter 2, and Deuteronomy 32:35. Already in 1522 in *A Sincere Admonition to All Chris-*

---

22. Thomas Müntzer, *Politische Schriften,* ed. C. Hinrichs, Hallische Monographien, vol. 17 (Halle, 1950), p. 73, *l.* 35 and p. 79, *l.* 144.

23. *WA* 30[II], 109, *ll.* 26–29; *LW* 46, 163.

24. J. Rühel to Luther, May 26, 1525, *WA* Briefe 3, 511, *ll.* 64 ff.

25. J. Cochläus, *Adverses latrocinantes et raptorias cohortes rusticorum Mart. Lutherus. Responsio* (1525).

tians to Guard Against Insurrection and Rebellion[26] Luther had mentioned these three passages together and thereby in a sense developed a scriptural basis for this topic.[27] They recur in the same sequence in his *Admonition to Peace*.[28] And in the brief span of his appeal *Against the Robbing and Murdering Hordes of Peasants,* verses from Romans 13 are quoted directly no fewer than seven times. Luther arrived at his assertions by exegeting these passages and applying their instruction to his situation. Today we may have a different opinion perhaps about those passages and their applicability. For Luther their unequivocal testimony permitted no discussion. Therefore every critique of Luther must go back to his scriptural teaching and concern itself with his exegesis, i.e., with his inability to see and acknowledge certain limitations to which the particular assertions of the Bible are also subject. Because in questions of authority, not only with regard to the state but likewise in the area of familial relations and the social structure of the entire populace, the Bible judged in one way and not in another, so did Luther. He did so without giving thought to possible hidden difficulties of a philosophical or social nature, such as the modern world has taught us to see. The majority of his contemporaries, however, also thought the way he did. Only a few succeeded in freeing themselves from these prescribed paths; the peasants, i.e., their leaders and programs, were not among those few at all or, at best, exhibited only weak tendencies in that direction.

It may be difficult for the modern critic to understand Luther in this regard. We are separated from Luther by the breakthrough from authoritarian to democratic principles. Instead of thinking in concepts of ruler and subject in a vertical system of elevation and subordination, we think in terms of a partnership of equal rights on a horizontal plane. From within our own framework, we may judge that something separates us

26. *WA* 8, (670) 676–87; *LW* 45, 57–74.
27. *WA* 8, 680, *ll.* 24 f./36 ff.; *LW* 45, 63.
28. *WA* 18, 303, *ll.* 16/32–304, *ll.* 4/22; et passim; *LW* 46, 25.

from Luther. But we cannot for this reason condemn Luther. To do so would mean applying standards to him and to his age that were first reached by modern men. We must conclude that, given Luther's situation and his day, it was hardly possible that he could do otherwise than impress on his congregation, and therefore on the peasants as well, the biblical assertion: Let everyone be subject to the authorities!

(2) This principle was the basis for all of Luther's further judgments on the matter. If this first, basically theological examination had thus already deprived the peasants' protest of every justification, then nothing essential could be changed by particular judgments. The issue was principally whether those same factual judgments were valid. The Peasants' War was the protest by a broad class of people against societal distresses, against societal abuses and in search of a far-reaching societal acceptance. "Societal" in this context refers not only to the specifically economic relationships between individual classes but also to the intellectual and legal dimensions of those relationships. Luther was to a large extent convinced of the factual justification for their complaints. At the beginning of his *Admonition to Peace* he addressed the authorities.[29] He introduced that address by establishing that this uprising could be blamed on no one but the princes and lords. Especially to blame were the bishops and monks, who had nothing else to do than to suppress the gospel and so to oppress their subjects with their worldly rule and to display such luxury that the poor man could no longer bear it. Basically they were not opposed by the peasants but by God himself. It would be good to yield to him, to stop blaming the gospel for the uprising and in active repentance to recognize the many legitimate peasant articles. Luther closed this section with the words: "And the people cannot tolerate it very long if their rulers set confiscatory tax rates and tax them out of their very skins. What good would it do a peasant if his field bore as many gulden as stalks of wheat if the rulers only taxed him all the more and then wasted it as

29. *WA* 18, 293–99; *LW* 46, 19–23.

though it were chaff to increase their luxury, and squandered his money on their own clothes, food, drink, and buildings? Would not the luxury and extravagant spending have to be checked so that a poor man could keep something for himself?"[30]

This section [of the *Admonition of Peace*] proves that Luther knew rather precisely what was at stake. This assertion is not contradicted by the entirely different tone that characterizes the subsequent, considerably more detailed section addressed to the peasants. There are good reasons for Luther's change in tone. First of all, in the section addressed to the peasants, nothing was rescinded, although only the first of the Twelve Articles —that the community should be authorized to choose its own minister—really withstood his critique. To him all the others, like the second article that dealt with the use of the required tithes, were either "nothing but theft and highway robbery,"[31] or were concerned with things which were not incumbent upon Luther, as "an evangelist."[32] There were books and regular courts of justice that dealt with such matters. Luther knew enough not to say much more than that concerning societal matters in his address to the peasants.

For, secondly, and this is now the deciding factor, even if the Articles were ever so just and right—as had been emphasized [by Luther] over against the Lords, for whom the Articles were really intended—they still lacked one most important thing: they appealed to a divine law but forgot the Christian law. "You have not been putting this program into effect by patiently praying to God, as Christians ought to do, but have instead undertaken to compel the rulers to give you what you wanted by using force and violence. This is against the law of the land and against natural justice."[33] Thereby Luther introduced a new concept that stood in direct opposition to the

30. *WA* 18, 299, *ll.* 7–12/25–30; *LW* 46, 23.
31. *WA* 18, 325, *ll.* 18 f./36 f.; *LW* 46, 38.
32. *WA* 18, 327, *ll.* 14/30; *LW* 46, 39.
33. *WA* 18, 319, *ll.* 11–14/28–31; *LW* 46, 34.

peasants' appeal to the divine law and in its own way spoke to the main question of the relation between the Peasants' War and the Reformation. For the issue was this: the Articles which had been put forward claimed to be Christian. What then was Christian about them? Luther said: Nothing! No factual justification could alter the fact that—considered in the light of the gospel—they were "selfish."[34] They appealed to the Scriptures to be sure. The peasants were happy to be called Christians. But what was here asserted and done in the name of the gospel had nothing to do with the gospel. It was only capable of discrediting the gospel as seditious among those who knew nothing of the true gospel. The Christian law is "not to strive against injustice, not to grasp the sword, not to protect ourselves, not to avenge ourselves, but to give up life and property, and let whoever takes it have it. . . . Suffering! suffering! Cross! cross! This and nothing else is the Christian law! But now you are fighting for temporal goods and will not let the coat go after the cloak, but want to recover the cloak. How then will you die and give up your life, or love your enemies and do good to them?"[35] Whoever wants to be a Christian must act in this way. Whoever will not conduct himself in this way should stop appealing to a Christian law. "However good and just your cause may be, nevertheless, because you would defend yourselves and are unwilling to suffer either violence or injustice, you may do anything that God does not prevent. However, leave the name Christian out of it. Leave the name Christian out, I say, and do not use it to cover up your impatient, disorderly, unchristian undertaking."[36] That was Luther's answer to the peasants' attempt to attach their cause to that of the Reformation.

(3) But this was not enough. Luther did not stop with taking the gospel away from the peasants and lowering their claim from the plane of "divine law" to the plane of temporal

34. *WA* 18, 298, *ll.* 10 f./28; *LW* 46, 22.
35. *WA* 18, 310, *ll.* 7–14/15–32; *LW* 46, 29.
36. *WA* 18, 314, *ll.* 9–14/28–32; *LW* 46, 31–32.

and natural law, i.e., he did not simply refer them away from himself to the appropriate courts of justice. On the contrary, Luther perceived the mark of the enthusiasts' misuse of the gospel in the peasants' appeal to it and in their attempt to understand the social question as a question and concrete task for faith. He was not satisfied with snatching the "name" of the gospel from the peasants and granting them civil self-vindication in its place. He labeled them with the heresy of enthusiasm.

It is Luther's thesis that the Peasants' War was a product of the "spirits of rebellion" and of Thomas Müntzer in particular. He could maintain that so directly[37] because an important phase of the war had occurred nearby under the immediate influence of Müntzer and his followers. Nevertheless, when he wrote the *Admonition to Peace* he had already been deeply convinced that powers were at work here that mouthed his good name and the cause of the gospel with no right and for nothing but show. For him the author of the Twelve Articles was "no godly and honest man,"[38] but a "lying preacher and false prophet."[39] For him there stood behind the movement "prophets of murder and spirits of rebellion,"[40] "spirits of murder,"[41] "mad prophets"[42] and "false prophets,"[43] as Luther emphasized in ever new variations, who "want to . . . become lords in the world."[44] Müntzer's direct intervention into events and the tragedy of Frankenhausen caused him to equate entirely "spirits of rebellion and insurgents."[45] The basis, however, for this blanket condemna-

37. In the treatise, "Eine schreckliche Geschichte und ein Gericht Gottes über Thomas Müntzer," *WA* 18, (362) 367–74. Cf. also *WA* 18, 357, *ll.* 13 ff.; *LW* 46, 49.
38. *WA* 18, 319, *ll.* 15/32; *LW* 46, 34.
39. *WA* 18, 326, *ll.* 11 f./29; *LW* 46, 38.
40. *WA* 18, 316, *ll.* 16 f./34; *LW* 46, 33. Cf. also *WA* 18, 301, *ll.* 2 f./ 20 f.; 308, *ll.* 2/20; *LW* 46, 24 and 28.
41. *WA* 18, 301, *ll.* 3/21; *LW* 46, 24.
42. *WA* 18, 311, *ll.* 2/21; *LW* 46, 29.
43. *WA* 18, 328, *ll.* 15/33; *LW* 46, 40.
44. *WA* 18, 308, *ll.* 3/21; *LW* 46, 28. Cf. *WA* 18, 328, *ll.* 15–18/33–36; *LW* 46, 40.
45. *WA* 18, 367, *l.* 10.

tion was simply that the action here being taken "in the name of the gospel,"[46] was like that for which Luther, years before, had already reproached the so-called Enthusiasts, chiefly in his treatise on *Temporal Authority*. His doctrine of the two kingdoms was here being disputed anew, and the contest was no longer merely theoretical but now eminently radical.[47] For him, this was evidence enough as to which spiritual leaders were responsible for the character of the entire movement. In his *Admonition to Peace* he wrote: "Anyone who reads through the chapters [of Scripture] cited [in the margin of the Twelve Articles] will realize that they speak very little in favor of what you are doing. On the contrary, they say that men should live and act like Christians." And he ended with the following: "He who seeks to use you to destroy the gospel is a prophet of discord."[48] Above all else, what was at stake for Luther was that here in the name of the gospel matters were proceeding not for, but in direct opposition to, the gospel. That meant, however, that they were also going against his own work; consequently, all those who were appealing specifically to him and to his co-workers could really do so only on the basis of hypocrisy. Therefore: "I must accept the fact that I am also involved in this struggle and consider you as enemies who, under the name of the gospel, act contrary to it, and want to do more to suppress my gospel than anything the pope and emperor have done to suppress it."[49]

In this way a wider line of separation was drawn. The "dear friends" and "dear brethren"[50] had become enemies with whom there could be no further fellowship. But this too was still not enough. To have been satisfied at this point would have meant

---

46. *WA* 18, 301, *ll.* 3/21. The phrase in question is omitted from the first complete sentence of *LW* 46, 24.

47. Cf. *WA* 18, 390, *ll.* 6 ff.; *LW* 46, 70.

48. *WA* 18, 320, *ll.* 2–6/18–22; *LW* 46, 35.

49. *WA* 18, 316, *ll.* 6–10/24–27; *LW* 46, 32.

50. E.g., *WA* 18, 299, *ll.* 16/34; 306, *ll.* 6/24; 308, *ll.* 1/19; *LW* 46, pp. 23, 27, and 28 (et passim) and *WA* 18, 301, *ll.* 14/32; *LW* 46, 24 (et passim).

remaining at the halfway mark. When one really thought it through to the end, the verdict of enthusiasm, and therefore of heresy, laid hold only of one side of the phenomenon. It laid hold only of the immanent dimension of an event that takes place essentially in transcendence. Luther drew the final decisive consequence: if the "spirits of rebellion" stand behind the peasants and their Articles, then they in turn are only tools in the hand of a mightier one, namely, the devil. Where else should the source of such a heresy be sought? Luther was deeply convinced that in the Peasants' War he was standing in a truly eschatological situation, where what was at stake under the superficial alternative for or against the peasants was the decision for or against God, for or against the gospel, for or against the devil.

If Luther had already stated this in his *Admonition to Peace*,[51] he strengthened his position in his treatise *Against the Robbing and Murdering Hordes of Peasants.* The following sentences, with their characteristic dependence upon Ephesians 6:12, reflect that strengthened position: "But if the ruler is a Christian and tolerates the gospel, so that the peasants have no appearance of a case against him, he should proceed with fear. . . . Then he should humbly pray for help against the devil, for we are contending not only 'against flesh and blood,' but 'against the spiritual hosts of wickedness in the air,' which must be attacked with prayer."[52] With reference to that, Walter Elliger writes: "For him (Luther) the political and social problem recedes completely behind the decisive judgment that the whole uprising in all its shabby and dazzling disguises is nothing but a refined attempt by Satan to seduce the cause of the gospel."[53]

51. *WA* 18, 316, *ll.* 14–17/32–35; *LW* 46, 33. Similarly, *WA* 18, 300, *ll.* 17/33–301, *ll.* 4/22; *LW* 46, 23 and 24; *WA* Briefe 3, 481, *ll.* 60–66.
52. *WA* 18, 359, *ll.* 26–33; *LW* 46, 52.
53. W. Elliger, *Luthers politisches Denken und Handeln* (Berlin, 1952), p. 71 (see pp. 69–74 for the complete account). The most recent treatment is M. Greschat, "Luthers Haltung im Bauernkrieg," in *Archiv für Reformationsgeschichte* 56 (1965): 31–47. Luther's position was "that of a Christian apocalypticist" (p. 32).

With that, however, Luther had abandoned the sphere of factual-historical considerations and set foot on a level where there is in the end no room for discussion. On that level the only thing at stake is whether or not one can adopt his view of history, unless of course all criticism of his position in the Peasants' War is to be renounced. But it should not be overlooked that Luther was saying nothing new in this case; he was reviewing long-established ideas already explained in *A Sincere Admonition*.[54]

In these charges of heresy and demonic influence there also lies the key for explaining the unprecedented severity of Luther's later opinions. On this level a neutral judgment concerning the facts of the matter, which aimed at an agreement, could no longer take place. Here the ultimate question of truth was posed, which in principle excluded every compromise. If Luther in his *Admonition to Peace* still wanted to give the peasants time to be converted and to accept an unequivocal position —either on the side of the gospel in the way he indicated or apart from the gospel in the fashion they had adopted—he very soon had to realize that such unequivocal clarity could no longer be attained. He had to realize that the peasants were continuing to mix the two positions as they had already. His *Admonition to Peace* came too late to be effective. The development had already advanced so far that unification along those lines was no longer possible. So it was only the next logical step when Luther then placed himself completely on the side of the authorities. In this respect he was not inconsistent. Whoever accused Luther of inconsistency—and quite a number of people did so even during his own time—had not read the *Admonition to Peace* very carefully.

Looking back from our vantage point, this unequivocal conclusion, so frightening and indeed even deadly in its severity, raises the question whether the particulars of Luther's judgment concerning the Peasants' War were ever really by them-

54. Cf. *WA* 8, 681, *ll*. 27–30; 683, *ll*. 26–33; 684, *l*. 14; *LW* 45, pp. 65, 68, and 69.

selves so correct, so in keeping with the subject, and so necessary, that together they actually allow only this one scathing judgment. We must understand clearly, however, that even Luther's later writings, especially his manifesto *Against the Robbing and Murdering Hordes of Peasants,* in no way influenced the outcome of the events. The later appeal to him by the lords and the polemics against him are all of a secondary nature. The princes had no need of such an admonition, even if Luther himself did boast on later occasions that more peasants had been slain with his writings than with the weapons of the princes.

IV

A. We begin with Luther's assessment of the Peasants' War as a social phenomenon in his reply to the lords and especially to the peasants. Let us try to clarify his point of view by citing the concrete example of Luther's response to the third of the Twelve Articles. That article demanded the abolition of serfdom on the basis of an appeal to the freedom for which Christ has set us free. Luther said in reply: "That is making Christian freedom a completely physical matter. Did not Abraham [Gen. 17:23] and other patriarchs . . . have slaves? Read what St. Paul teaches about servants, who, at that time, were all slaves. This article, therefore, absolutely contradicts the gospel. It proposes robbery, for it suggests that every man should take his body away from his lord, even though his body is the lord's property. A slave can be a Christian, and have Christian freedom. . . . This article would make all men equal, and turn the spiritual kingdom of Christ into a worldly, external kingdom; and that is impossible. A worldly kingdom cannot exist without an inequality of persons, some being free, some imprisoned, some lords, some subjects."[55]

Undoubtedly Luther was right when he denied the peasants their claim to freedom on that basis. In point of fact, things

55. *WA* 18, 326, *ll.* 15/33–327, *ll.* 8/24; *LW* 46, 39.

here were mixed together that had nothing really to do with each other. Nevertheless, Luther's reply is not satisfactory. Basically he was just as guilty of the charge he was leveling at the peasants. His allusion to Paul and the Patriarchs in fact lays hold of only one strand of the biblical testimony, over against which there stands another. The social legislation of the Old Testament drew clear boundaries, and the New Testament is also acquainted with other voices, however controversial the Epistle to Philemon in particular may be.[56] But, using the Bible to argue in this way, Luther accomplished no more and no less than to employ Scripture to bind the Christian of a much later age to the pagan social structures of antiquity. Luther was correct when he said that a Christian *can* live as a slave without detriment to his faith but incorrect when he inferred that slavery *must* therefore continue. To assert that contributes substantially to the formation of an external order on the basis of an appeal to the Bible. But because Luther found this order in existence already, the situation was quite different for him than if his concern had been to effect something entirely new and entirely without precedent. Because the Bible presupposes this social order, Luther also defended it by a biblicistic appeal to the Scriptures. He did so without recognizing that basically the problem he faced was theological only in a very limited sense, or at best was theological only to the extent that it meant considering where the obligations begin and end in this matter and whether the problem does not really have two sides. Because the question has two sides one may inquire not only whether a Christian can be a slave but also whether a Christian may in good conscience own slaves. To be sure, Paul Althaus in his study of *Luthers Haltung im Bauernkrieg*[57] ("Luther's Conduct in the Peasants' War") claims that in Luther's view of slavery

56. According to Luther's interpretation, it did not speak against him. Cf. *WA* 25, 76 f., especially p. 77, *ll.* 3 ff.: "Non vult eum eximere a servitute" (1527).

57. P. Althaus, *Luthers Haltung im Bauernkrieg. Ein Beitrag zur lutherischen Sozialethik* (Darmstadt, 1962).

there is an emphasis on the "Christian-social duties of the strong."[58] Yet no trace of that is to be found here. Here there is no mention of one's duties to his brothers or the like. This is true not only in regard to this point [i.e., Luther's response to Article 3 of the Twelve Articles] but in regard to the entire literature concerning the Peasants' War.

This is just the place to begin anew our critique relative to Luther's criticism of the movement as a social phenomenon, on the one hand, and the question of its relation to the Reformation, on the other. It is true that formally Luther was correct when he denied the peasants the right to base their demands on the gospel and referred them instead to regular courts of law. This reprimand, however, had truly only a *pro forma* value. Practically speaking, this way was not accessible to the subjects. But the problem reaches still further and still deeper: though the peasants' slogan referring to the divine law may have arisen even before the Reformation and outside the official church, though it therefore may have had a very definite theological tendency, and though Luther could also justly contend that in this context an appeal to him was absolutely impossible, it was still through his influence and through the advance of the Reformation that this slogan had first become a "catchword arousing the masses."[59] It is very questionable whether Luther was so clearly justified in degrading the powerful religious impulses that stood behind this watchword and, further, whether his axiom opposing every attempt to understand and employ the gospel as a social agent can be carried through with this sort of radicality. For here two sides can again be seen. I mean, of course, that corresponding to the reprimand directed at the peasants there should have been a clear warning directed at the lords. They should have been warned to do what justice obviously demanded and beyond that to do those additional things Christian love expects, a love even the princes pretended to follow. In the case of Luther, however, we seek in vain for such a

58. Ibid., p. 183, note 1.
59. Franz, *Der deutsche Bauernkrieg*, p. 90.

warning or find it at best only in insignificant statements. Luther addressed both sides, it is true, but he spoke to each with very different emphases and his statements remained almost completely negative. He very consciously refrained from telling the lords what their actions as Christians should have been. I believe he ought to have told them. Others did so. I will mention only the opinion written by Brenz, the reformer from Schwäbisch-Hall, concerning the Twelve Articles and that by Urbanus Rhegius from Augsburg concerning the Memmingen Articles. Next to the position papers by Luther and Melanchthon these two documents are the most extensive and most significant comments by the Reformation concerning the general course of events. Brenz and Rhegius did what Luther failed to do. They did not abandon the least little part of the Reformation outlook. For them, too, it was a foregone conclusion that the peasants carried their claims beyond the limits set by the gospel. But the claims and demands they had to deny the peasants, they placed on the conscience of the lords as a clear Christian duty; the lords could in no way exempt their own rule from the principle of Christian corporate life, i.e., from the principle of love. With this attitude Rhegius wrote an opinion concerning serfdom, and Luther made use of it in his *Admonition to Peace*. A generous interpretation would assert that by doing so he adopted it as his own and meant to do just that. This does not seem to me to be very probable. Brenz and Rhegius did what was, in my opinion, really necessary: not only did they declare that they themselves were responsible, but they also held the view that specifically the gospel could offer a solution to the problem at hand, a solution meeting the demands of all interested parties. They were of the opinion that with regard to concrete questions the gospel sanctions a Christian answer that goes beyond a general, i.e. nonobligatory, admonition to both parties. Therefore, in Brenz's discussion of each of the Twelve Articles, he directed both the peasants and the lords to the duties they each had if they wanted to be Christians. Rhegius did the same kind of thing. In this way they achieved two results: on the one hand, a factually much more positive evaluation of the peasant demands—even though, in complete agreement with Luther, they totally rejected any allegedly Christian law—and, on the other hand, a significantly more effective, because more pointed, admonition to the lords. They reprimanded the peasants for the claims they based on Christianity, such as the demand to be released from serfdom, and at the same time admonished the lords to free their subjects as an expression of Christian love. It is significant that both men, Brenz explicitly and Rhegius at least implicitly, emphasized the possibility, if not also the necessity, of Christian lords being guided in their rule by God's word. For Luther, on the other hand, a godly prince was a "rare bird"[60] and governing with the gospel a utopian notion, if not just enthusiasm.

B. The very fact that Luther saw his own theological position under attack led him to see in this the marks of heresy completely realized, and he reacted by assuming a definite position. We must ask what should be retained from that position. No one is in doubt about the possibility of such a judgment. The problem lies in the question of its necessity: Was the situation in fact so clear theologically that the question of truth had to be formulated with such severity? One's answer will depend on how far he is prepared to follow Luther's theological presuppositions. It will depend on whether one agrees with him that *"Christus non curat politiam aut oeconomiam,"*[61] or whether, on the contrary, one is convinced that obedience to the gospel makes it impossible to ignore current social problems. Therefore I will not answer this question here. The whole complex of issues has yet another aspect. That is to say, when Luther labeled the peasant movement as enthusiastic, he was also delivering a quasi-historical assessment of the situation; he was asserting the dependence of the peasants on sharply defined, theological, anti-Reformation power groups. The sources that we know he was acquainted with, however, left Luther

60. *WA* 11, 267, *ll.* 30 f.
61. See above, note 19.

really unprepared to give such a general verdict. He probably did not know, for example, who the leaders of the peasants in South Germany were. It is quite unlikely that—at the time when he wrote his *Admonition to Peace*—he knew anything about the role played by the Memmingen preacher Christoph Schappeler, by Balthasar Hubmaier, or by the emerging Anabaptist movement, whose role in any case cannot be clearly sketched even today. It is much more likely that Luther simply generalized the obviously visible example provided by Müntzer and transferred it to the movement in general. The point of similarity was the fact that the principal document of the insurrections, namely, the Twelve Articles, disclosed a spirit theologically repugnant to his own. It was in this way that Luther formed a specific judgment, not so much historical as systematic, which found the movement guilty of "enthusiasm" and a "spirit of rebellion" and therefore "heresy." However, the Peasants' War was not a work of the "enthusiasts," the "spirits of rebellion," or "prophets of murder," and also only partially that of Thomas Müntzer. Luther's generalization made his judgment factually wrong, however much justification he may have had for it on a theological level. And Luther overlooked the fact that he had thereby ventured much too far and become much too partisan to be able on this basis to mediate between the factions. The tools of the devil cannot be handled objectively!

Let us glance again at the South and the regions where little was known of Thomas Müntzer. There every attempt like that of Luther to discredit the movement theologically fails at once. There, too, the problem caused the reform movement by the peasants' appeal to the gospel was well known. With as much decisiveness as Luther, the reformers of the South German cities and provinces protested against this appeal by the peasants. They characterized it as a misuse and perversion of the gospel. But they refrained from drawing any further conclusions. The emphasis on fanaticism was completely absent from their assessments of the situation. Evidently they were unconvinced of the necessity of going to such lengths on that point.

In view of this it also scarcely requires specific mention that all eschatological or even apocalyptic features are lacking in the South German interpretation of these events. Luther's interpretation of contemporary events as a struggle between God and Satan in which the work of the Reformation was in a very real sense at stake, was completely foreign to them. Even the idea that the devil stood behind the peasants was missing. The insurrections were understood without exception within the dimension of immanence; they were understood from within the social situation; and the theological aspect was restricted to parrying the improper use of the gospel by the peasants on the one hand and, on the other hand, indicating the decisive impulse of the gospel for solving the problems they faced. This way of looking at things was evidently the basis for the marked superiority of the opinions by the reformers from the South German centers of insurrection. This orientation gave them a high degree of objectivity and insight into the situation and the possibilities available as well; it revealed workable methods for accomplishing the tasks, methods which were not adopted everywhere to be sure, but which nonetheless could occasionally contribute something essential. Above all, however, it prevented any further hardening of positions through [the inclusion of] elements not primarily inherent in the insurrections themselves. If, by means of his *Admonition to Peace,* Luther also wanted to prepare the way for a friendly agreement—on the basis of that *Admonition*—such an agreement would not have been possible. Brenz and Rhegius offered it. Brenz came too late with his opinion. The Diet of Heidelberg, to which he was to deliver the material, did not take place, because the elector had chosen no longer to negotiate but rather to attempt a more radical "solution" with weapons. But Rhegius attained his goal. He evidently found the appropriate partners in the Council of Memmingen and the peasant leaders of his region. On the basis of the Memmingen Articles a peaceful agreement was reached there: serfdom was abolished, the choice of the pastor conceded (although with several limitations), and free hunting and fishing allowed. Only the decision about the tithe was tabled. The success of this sensible behavior was apparent. Although the territory of the imperial city of Memmingen lay in the center of the South German insurrections, it alone remained undisturbed.

This example demonstrates with sufficient clarity what possibilities were truly available; it demonstrates what positive results the entire movement could have produced, provided only that the appropriate powers on all sides had pushed the movement forward: the peasants and government as well as the preachers whose advice still meant a great deal. On the part of the Reformation—I cannot put it otherwise—a great opportunity was lost. I certainly do not mean the opportunity to place itself at the head of the insurgents, in order, together with the peasants' revolution, to achieve a final victory for the cause of the Reformation. This can be maintained only by someone who does not at all recognize what was at stake for Luther and his co-workers. The opportunity was rather accepting and using the task of the mediator and expert, a task that had been proposed to them by both sides, as earnestly as the situation allowed and demanded in order to avert the menacing tragedy. This would have meant developing, with a clear eye for the facts and a correspondingly moderate understanding of the gospel, standards able to meet the demands of justice for both sides—for the authorities as the forces of order as well as for the subjects striving for their rights; it would have meant, therefore, truly rising above the factions with warning, admonition, and guidance. The few who attained such a level unfortunately did not prevail; otherwise some things could have been prevented and many things accomplished. Either their opinions came too late, so that developments had already moved in another direction, or they preached to deaf ears. Again the example of Memmingen remains isolated, as does that of Strassburg, where the three reformed preachers Capito, Bucer, and Zell decisively influenced the politics of the city. But to desire to scold the other reformers and above all Luther for being slaves of the princes would mean possessing as little historical sense even today as possessed by some critics of that time. If we want to reproach Luther today, then we should reproach him only with the following: that he did not assess the situation moderately enough; and that with his religious overevaluation of the movement, as a result of generalizing his own experiences, he imported an essentially alien element into the matter, and in this way laid a foundation that left no room for an objective appraisal. He shared his attitude towards the authorities with the majority of his contemporaries. In many other ways he surpassed them completely. That the princes utilized his opinions for their own purposes cannot be held against him.

For Further Reading

SOURCE MATERIAL:

LUTHER, MARTIN. "Admonition to Peace, A Reply to the Twelve Articles of the Peasants in Swabia." *Luther's Works* 46, (3) 17–43. Edited by Robert C. Schultz. Philadelphia: Fortress Press, 1967.

LUTHER, MARTIN. "Against the Robbing and Murdering Hordes of Peasants." *Luther's Works* 46, (45) 49–55.

LUTHER, MARTIN. "An Open Letter on the Harsh Book Against the Peasants." *Luther's Works* 46, (57) 63–85.

BOEHMER, HEINRICH, ed. *Urkunden zur Geschichte des Bauernkrieges und der Wiedertäufer.* Kleine Texte für theologische und philologische Vorlesungen und Übungen, vol. 50–51. Bonn: A. Marcus und E. Weber's Verlag, 1910; Berlin, 1933.

ZÖLLNER, W., ed. *Zur Geschichte des grossen deutschen Bauernkrieges. Dokumente und Materialien.* Berlin, 1961.

GENERAL READING:

BAINTON, ROLAND. *Here I Stand.* New York: Abingdon Press, 1950.

WARD, A. W.; PROTHERO, G.; and LEATHES, S., eds. *The Reformation.* Cambridge Modern History, vol. II. New York: Macmillan Company, 1904.

CRANZ, F. EDWARD. *An Essay on the Development of Luther's Thought on Justice, Law, and Society.* Cambridge, Mass.: Harvard University Press, 1959.

GRITSCH, ERIC W. *Reformer Without a Church: The Life and Thought of Thomas Muentzer 1488(?)–1525.* Philadelphia: Fortress Press, 1967.

HOLBORN, HAJO. *A History of Modern Germany: The Reformation.* New York: Alfred Knopf, 1959.

SCHAPIRO, JACOB S. *Social Reform and the Reformation.* New York: Columbia University Press, 1909.

SCHWIEBERT, E. G. *Luther and His Times.* St. Louis: Concordia Publishing House, 1950.

TRINKAUS, CHARLES. "The Religious Foundations of Luther's Social Views." In *Essays in Medieval Life and Thought,* edited by John H. Mundy, Richard W. Emery, and Benjamin N. Nelson, pp. 71–87. New York: Columbia University Press, 1955.

THE PEASANTS' WAR:

ALTHAUS, PAUL. *Luthers Haltung im Bauernkrieg. Ein Beitrag zur lutherischen Sozialethik.* Darmstadt: Wissenschaftliche Buchgesellschaft, 1962.

BAX, E. B. *The Peasants War in Germany, 1525–26.* New York: Russell and Russell, 1968.

CROSSLEY, R. N. "Luther and the Peasants' War: A Brief Summary." In *The Dawn of Modern Civilization,* edited by K. Strand. Ann Arbor: University of Michigan Press, 1962.

ENGELS, FRIEDRICH. *The Peasant War in Germany.* New York: International Publishers, 1926.

FRANZ, G. *Der deutsche Bauernkrieg.* Darmstadt: H. Gentner, 1956.

GRIMM, HAROLD J. "Luther, Luther's Critics and the Peasant Revolt." *Lutheran Church Quarterly* 19 (1946): 115–32.

LAU, FRANZ. "Der Bauernkrieg und das angebliche Ende der lutherischen Reformation als spontaner Volksbewegung." *Luther-Jahrbuch* 26 (1959): 109–34.

MACKENSEN, HEINZ F. "Historical Interpretation and Luther's Role in the Peasant Revolt." *Concordia Theological Monthly* 35 (1964): 197–209.

SESSIONS, KYLE, ed. *Reformation and Authority: The Meaning of the Peasants' Revolt.* Lexington, Mass.: Heath, 1968.

SOLLE, R. W. *Reformation und Revolution. Der deutsche Bauernkrieg und Luthers Stellung in demselben.* Halle: Verein für Reformationsgeschichte, 1897.

STOLZE, W. *Bauernkrieg und Reformation.* Leipzig: M. Heinsius Nachfolger, Eger und Sievers, 1926.

Facet Books Already Published

Historical Series:

1. *Were Ancient Heresies Disguised Social Movements?*
   by A. H. M. Jones. 1966
2. *Popular Christianity and the Early Theologians*
   by H. J. Carpenter. 1966
3. *Tithing in the Early Church*
   by Lukas Vischer (translated by Robert C. Schultz). 1966
4. *Jerusalem and Rome*
   by Hans von Campenhausen and Henry Chadwick. 1966
5. *The Protestant Quest for a Christian America 1830–1930*
   by Robert T. Handy. 1967
6. *The Formation of the American Catholic Minority 1820–1860*
   by Thomas T. McAvoy. 1967
7. *A Critical Period in American Religion 1875–1900*
   by Arthur M. Schlesinger, Sr. 1967
8. *Images of Religion in America*
   by Jerald C. Brauer. 1967
9. *The American Religious Depression 1925–1935*
   by Robert T. Handy. 1968
10. *The Origins of Fundamentalism: Toward a Historical Interpretation*
    by Ernest R. Sandeen. 1968
11. *The Idea of Progress in American Protestant Thought 1930–1960*
    by Paul A. Carter. 1969
12. *The Problem of Christian Unity in Early Nineteenth-Century America*
    by Lefferts A. Loetscher. 1969

Biblical Series:

Social Ethics Series:

1. *Our Calling*
   by Einar Billing (translated by Conrad Bergendoff). 1965
2. *The World Situation*
   by Paul Tillich. 1965
3. *Politics as a Vocation*
   by Max Weber (translated by H. H. Gerth and C. Wright Mills). 1965
4. *Christianity in a Divided Europe*
   by Hanns Lilje. 1965
5. *The Bible and Social Ethics*
   by Hendrik Kraemer. 1965
6. *Christ and the New Humanity*
   by C. H. Dodd. 1965
7. *What Christians Stand For in the Secular World*
   by William Temple. 1965
8. *Legal Responsibility and Moral Responsibility*
   by Walter Moberly. 1965
9. *The Divine Command: A New Perspective on Law and Gospel*
   by Paul Althaus (translated by Franklin Sherman). 1966
10. *The Road to Peace*
    by John C. Bennett, Kenneth Johnstone, C. F. von Weizsäcker, Michael Wright. 1966
11. *The Idea of a Natural Order: With an Essay on Modern Asceticism*
    by V. A. Demant. 1966
12. *Kerygma, Eschatology, and Social Ethics*
    by Amos N. Wilder. 1966
13. *Affluence and the Christian*
    by Hendrik van Oyen (translated by Frank Clarke). 1966
14. *Luther's Doctrine of the Two Kingdoms*
    by Heinrich Bornkamm (translated by Karl H. Hertz). 1966
15. *Christian Decision in the Nuclear Age*
    by T. R. Milford. 1967
16. *Law and Gospel*
    by Werner Elert (translated by Edward H. Schroeder). 1967
17. *On Marriage*
    by Karl Barth (translated by A. T. Mackay *et al.*). 1968